OREGON TRAIL

SOUVENIR BOOK

Rick Steber - Writing

Don Gray - Illustrations

ISBN 0-945134-97-5

Library of Congress Cataloging in Publication Data
Steber, Rick, 1946 —
Writing: R. Steber; artwork: D. Gray
    SUMMARY: An overview of the Oregon Trail
including some excerpts from diaries.
    1. Oregon Trail.   2. Overland journeys to the
Pacific. 3. Pioneers — The West

BONANZA PUBLISHING • PRINEVILLE, OREGON

THE OREGON TRAIL

In the early 1800s wandering mountain men, searching for new trading and trapping territories, helped to establish the path that became the Oregon Trail.

Men like William Ashley, Jedediah Smith, Jim Bridger, John Colter, Robert Stuart, Wilson Price Hunt, Joe Meek, Kit Carson and many others explored this route of least resistance across the North American continent. They followed buffalo trails and paths of commerce established by Native Americans from the Missouri River up the Platte and Sweetwater rivers, over the Rocky Mountains at South Pass to the Great Basin and beyond, to the Pacific Northwest or to California.

The eastern portion of the trail was well-traveled by fur company wagons supplying the trappers. In 1832 fur trader and soldier of fortune Captain Benjamin Bonneville extended the road by taking wagons as far as Green River (Wyoming). Four years later missionary Dr. Marcus Whitman and his associates lengthened the trail even farther by bringing a two-wheeled cart to the Hudson's Bay Company post at Fort Boise (Idaho).

In 1840 the Reverends Harvey Clark and Alvin Smith, layman P.B. Littlejohn and their wives started west to build a mission. They brought their wagons as far as Fort Hall (Idaho) where they traded them to a group of trappers.

One of the trappers, Robert Newell, gave an account of their attempt to extend the wagon road to Oregon: *"Our animals began to fail, we began to lighten up, finally threw away our wagon beds, and* were quite sorry we had undertaken the job.... In a rather rough and reduced state we arrived at Dr. Whitman's mission station, in the Walla Walla valley (Washington).... On hearing me regret that we had ever undertaken to bring the wagons the Doctor said: 'Oh, you will never regret it; you have broken the ice and when others see that wagons have passed they, too, will pass and in a few years the valley will be full of our people.'"

In May 1842 a wagon train consisting
of 105 men, women and children, 18 ox-
drawn wagons and a considerable band
of horses, mules and cattle departed from
Elm Grove, Missouri. At Green River
some of the wagons were dismantled and
used to make pack saddles. The remain-
ing wagons were left at Fort Hall and the

emigrants continued on horseback and afoot to the Willamette Valley of Oregon.

Historians recognize 1843 as the official beginning of the Oregon Trail. That spring a group of nearly a thousand men, women and children, 120 wagons, and 5,000 head of cattle assembled at Elm Grove. They were there for many reasons. Some were born wanderers, comfortable only on the outer fringes of the frontier. Others were attracted by the potential of the western region; the chance to forge a new life and the opportunity, if the Congress passed a bill before it, of owning a free section of farm land. All they had to do was go west to claim it.

Along the Platte River the pioneers were overtaken by Dr. Whitman who was returning from the east coast to his mission in the Oregon country. He was welcomed into the company as an advisor because of his experience in crossing the continent. He helped choose camp sites and spent much of his time scouting the best route for the wagons, plunging his horse into streams in search of fords and meeting with bands of roving Indians.

One of the emigrants, James W. Nesmith, wrote: *"Dr. Marcus Whitman was not a regular clergyman.... While with us he was clad entirely in buckskin ... he said more to us about the practical matters connected with our march than he did about theology or religious creeds."*

At Fort Hall some of the pioneers abandoned their wagons but others, encouraged by Dr. Whitman, continued on. The company broke apart at the Whitman Mission. Some went horseback or afoot along the Indian trail hugging the south bank of the Columbia River while others built flat-bottomed boats and floated the dangerous river.

The Oregon Trail was never a well-defined highway running from east to west. It was a wide trail that followed the lay of the land and a series of landmarks. On the flats wagon drivers spread out so they would not have to eat so much dust; but there were natural bottle-necks that forced the wagons into single file. In these places the iron-rimmed wheels wore ruts two-feet deep in solid rock.

Diaries kept by Oregon Trail pioneers tell the story of the crossing in human terms: of leaving family and friends, making do with only the bare essentials, cooking over a buffalo chip fire, confrontations with Indians, being trapped in buffalo stampedes, suffering from the heat and cold and wild swings in weather, accidents, sickness, death.

The voices of the pioneers spoke of the hardships of six months on a road that stretched 2,000 rugged miles. They could never linger over a grave or beside a grassy riverbank because if winter came early, before they crossed the Cascades or Sierra Nevada, they would have to abandon their wagons and belongings and try to get through on foot.

The heyday of the trail occurred after gold was discovered in California in 1848. During the next few decades it is estimated that 300,000 people came west over the Oregon Trail. Travel became so heavy pioneers complained it was like one continuous wagon train snaking its way west. Their stock over-grazed a forty-mile swath, great numbers of buffalo, antelope and rabbits were killed for food and, because of unsanitary camping conditions, the pioneers suffered from epidemics of cholera and mountain fever.

During one year, 1852, it was estimated that one out of every ten pioneers died. Diaries reveal that from Platte River (Nebraska) to Fort Laramie (Wyoming), a distance of 400 miles, there was an average of twelve graves to the mile.

Aside from disease, the major cause of death on the way west was from accidental shooting because the pioneers always kept their rifles loaded and at the ready for hunting and protection. Contrary to

common belief, comparatively few
emigrants were killed by Indians.

In 1869 the transcontinental railroad
was completed to California. In 1883 rail
service reached the Northwest. But many
west-bound settlers could not afford the
cost of renting a railroad car to transport
their belongings. Travel over the Oregon
Trail, and the California Cut-Off,
continued until the automobile became
common in the 1920s.

The Route of the Oregon Trail

THE JOURNEY WEST

In early spring pioneers gathered and formed wagon trains for the trip west, setting up temporary camps near Council Bluffs, Elk Grove, Independence, Liberty, Nebraska City, St. Joseph, Weston, Westport and other established towns that lined the Missouri River.

JUMPING OFF
"I well remember what a hullabaloo the neighbors set up when father said we were going to Oregon. They told him his family would all be killed by the Indians, or if we escaped the Indians we could either starve to death or drown or be lost in the desert, but father was not much of a hand to draw back after he had put his hand to the plow, so he went ahead and made ready for the trip." (BENJAMIN FRANKLIN BONNEY, 1845)

"The allowance of provisions for each grown person, to make the journey from the Missouri River to California, should suffice for 110 days. The following is deemed requisite, viz.: 150 lbs. of flour, or its equivalent in hard bread; 25 lbs. of bacon or pork, and enough fresh beef to be driven on the hoof to make up the meat component of the ration; 15 lbs. of coffee, and 25 lbs. of sugar; also a quantity of saleratus or yeast powders for making bread, and salt and pepper. These are the chief articles of subsistence necessary for the trip, and they should be used with economy, reserving a good portion for the western half of the journey.

"I once traveled with a party of New Yorkers in route for California. They were perfectly ignorant of every thing relating to this kind of campaigning, and had overloaded their wagons with almost every thing except the very articles most important and necessary; the consequence was, that they exhausted their teams, and were obliged to throw away the greater part of their loading. They soon learned that Champagne, East India sweetmeats, olives, etc., etc., were not the most useful articles for a prairie tour." (RANDOLPH MARCY, THE PRAIRIE TRAVELER, A HANDBOOK FOR OVERLAND EXPEDITIONS, 1859)

COURTHOUSE ROCK

"We spent an hour on the summit writing. Our heads became dizzy, we began to hunt the base and had a hard time to overtake our wagons which we could only see by the dust they raised; and being nearly fifteen miles off we traveled hard but did not overtake them until they camped for the night. We had left camp without a gun, pistol or knife, which we ought to have had as the wolves and bears became unusually thick before we got in." (WALTER G. PIGMAN, 1850)

CHIMNEY ROCK

"This afternoon we sighted at a distance the so-called Chimney Rock ... nothing new otherwise ... killed a cow today and the meat was cut up into very thin slices. They are hung around to dry and look like red curtins...." (CHARLES PREUSS, 1842)

SCOTT'S BLUFF

"(Scott's) Bluff looks like an old castle with a rounding top and several others similar in line like a number of very large buildings." (ASAHEL MUNGER, 1839)

FORT LARAMIE

"Our camp is stationary; part of the emigrants are trading at the fort where items sell at high prices. In the afternoon we gave the Indians a feast, and held a long talk with them. Each family ... contributed a portion of bread, meat, coffee or sugar, which being cooked, a table was set by spreading buffalo skins upon the ground...." (JOEL PALMER, 1845)

"The road is strewn with articles thrown away.... I recognize the trunks of some of the passengers who had accompanied me from St. Louis to Kansas, on the Missouri, and who had here thrown away their wagons and everything they could not pack." (CAPT. HOWARD STANSBURY, 1852)

INDEPENDENCE ROCK

"Independence Rock is the great register of the desert; the names of all the travelers who have passed by are there to be read, written in coarse character; mine figures among them." (FR. PIERRE-JEAN DESMET, 1840)

SOUTH PASS

"From South Pass the nature of our journeying changed, and assumed the character of a retreat, a disastrous, ruinous retreat. Oxen and horses began to perish in large numbers; often falling dead in their yokes in the road. The heat-dried wagon, striking on rocks, would fall to pieces...." (GEORGE B. CURREY, 1853)

"The Wind River range of mountains, abutting on our right loom out almost over our trail...." (S.H. TAYLOR, 1853)

"I am weary of this journey. I long for the quiet of home where I can be at peace once more...." (AGNES STEWART, 1853)

FORT BRIDGER

"I have established a small fort, with black-smith shop and a supply of iron, in the road of the immigrants on Black Fork and Green River. In coming out the immigrants are generally well supplied with money, but by the time they get here they are in need of all kinds of supplies, horses, provisions, smith-work, etc...." (JAMES BRIDGER, 1843)

"It (Fort Bridger) is built of poles and daubed with mud; it is a shabby concern." (JOEL PALMER, 1846)

SNAKE RIVER

"The country all the way down the Snake River is one of the most desolate and dreary waste in the world.... The dust is here so light that it sometimes raises 300 feet above the wagon train." (E.S. McCOMAS, 1862)

POWDER RIVER VALLEY

"Came 19 miles over a rough, dusty road. Came to Powder River valley. This is a delightful valley of fine grass, and good water. Saw the Blue Mountains in the distance covered with pine.... It is so cold that we are all shivering with our thick clothes on. Have nothing for fire but green willow branches." (ESTHER BELLE MCMILLAN, 1852)

BLUE MOUNTAINS

"The timber had to be cut and removed to make way for the wagons. The trees were cut just near enough to the ground to allow the wagons to pass over the stumps and the road through the forest was only cleared out wide enough for a wagon to pass along .... we were overtaken by a snow storm which made the prospect very dismal. I remember wading through mud and snow and suffering from the cold and wet...." (JESSE APPLEGATE, 1843)

CASCADE MOUNTAINS

*"Had a superb view of the Cascade Moun-
tains. To the west, Mt. Hood, the loftiest of these,
was very visible and being covered with snow
with the sun shining upon it, it looked like a golden
cloud in the distance, being 150 miles away!"*
(ESTHER MCMILLAN HANNA, 1852)

WILLAMETTE VALLEY

*"Here we are at last in Oregon City, that long-
looked for place!"* (ESTHER BELLE MCMILLAN, 1852)

*"The environs of our new home, surrounded
by giant fir trees, the healthful sea breezes, the
strange sights and sounds were sources of*

continual thought. The long distance that separated us from our old home in the Mississippi valley, precluded any form of home sickness and our united efforts were wholly set upon the building of a home." (SARAH CUMMINS, 1845)

NACHES PASS

"Welcome news reached us that a party of workmen started out to make a road for us through Naches Pass over the Cascades.... At Summit Hill we spliced rope and prepared for the steep descent which we saw before us. One end of the rope was fastened to the axles of the wagons, the other end thrown around a tree and held by our men...." (JAMES LONGMIRE, 1853)

CALIFORNIA CUT-OFF

California-bound emigrants shared the same route west as the Oregon-bound emigrants. At some point they would reach a parting of the ways. The most popular cut-off was at the Raft River Crossing. Here those bound for California followed the Raft River valley and eventually they crossed the Sierra Nevada.

As with the Oregon Trail, the California Cut-Off contributed to the settlement of the west. It is estimated that between 1840 and 1860, more than 250,000 emigrants used the California Cut-Off trail while about 50,000 continued on to Oregon.

"*At Fort Hall we were met by Caleb Greenwood... an old mountain man employed by Captain Sutter to come to Fort Hall to divert the Oregon-bound emigrants to California.... He told us that while no emigrants had as yet gone to California, there was an easy grade and crossing the mountains would not be difficult. He said that Capt. Sutter would have men meet the emigrants who would go and that Sutter would supply them with plenty of potatoes, coffee and dried beef. He also said ... that to every head of a family who would settle near Sutter's Fort, Captain Sutter would give six sections of land of his Spanish land grant....*" (BENJAMIN FRANKLIN BONNEY, 1846)

"We did not ask you white men to come here. The Great Spirit gave us this country as a home. You had yours. We did not interfere with you. The Great Spirit gave us plenty of land to live on, and buffalo, deer, antelope and other game. But you have come here; you are taking my land from me; you are killing off our game, so it is hard for us to live. Now, you tell us to work for a living, but the Great Spirit did not make us to work, but to live by hunting. You white men can work if you want to. We do not interfere with you, and again you say, why do you not become civilized: We do not want your civilization! We would live as our fathers did, and their fathers before them." (CRAZY HORSE, OGLALA SIOUX CHIEF)

Tales of the Wild West

The TALES OF THE WILD WEST is a continuing series that dramatically portrays the many facets of Western settlement.

Collect the entire series in perfectbound, hardbound, and cassette tape.

Current Titles

Oregon Trail	*Miners*
Pacific Coast	*Grandpa's Stories*
Indians	*Pioneers*
Cowboys	*Campfire Stories*
Women of the West	*Tall Tales*
Children's Stories	*Gunfighters*
Loggers	*Grandma's Stories*
Mountain Men	

Ask your local retailer for these titles. Or request a free catalog by writing:

Bonanza Publishing • Box 204 • Prineville, OR 97754

For more information about the Oregon Trail, and the Western frontier, read these other books by Rick Steber.

Last of the Pioneers: Pioneers traveled the Oregon Trail in covered wagons as late as the 1920s. This little-known era of history is told in the pioneers' own words.

Roundup: A major contribution toward preserving western history and celebrating the lives and work of horse people.

Heartwood: People from a simpler time reflect on their values and the ethics of hard work, vividly explaining how they overcame adversity and found happiness in a life well lived.

New York to Nome, The Northwest Passage by Canoe: The true adventure of the 1936-1937 expedition to discover the Northwest Passage.

Wild Horse Rider: A biography of 1912 World Saddlebronc Champion, Lew Minor.